T0151197

The Conscience

Inner Land

A Guide into the Heart of the Gospel

■ □ □ □ □   **The Inner Life**
The Inner Life
The Heart
Soul and Spirit

□ ■ □ □ □   **The Conscience**
The Conscience and Its Witness
The Conscience and Its Restoration

□ □ ■ □ □   **Experiencing God**
The Experience of God
The Peace of God

□ □ □ ■ □   **Fire and Spirit**
Light and Fire
The Holy Spirit

□ □ □ □ ■   **The Living Word**

Volume 2

The Conscience

Eberhard Arnold

PLOUGH PUBLISHING HOUSE

Published by Plough Publishing House
Walden, New York, USA
Robertsbridge, East Sussex, UK
Elsmore, NSW, Australia

Plough is the publishing house of the Bruderhof, an international community of families and singles seeking to follow Jesus together. Members of the Bruderhof are committed to a way of radical discipleship in the spirit of the Sermon on the Mount. Inspired by the first church in Jerusalem (Acts 2 and 4), they renounce private property and share everything in common in a life of nonviolence, justice, and service to neighbors near and far. To learn more about the Bruderhof's faith, history, and daily life, see Bruderhof.com.

Translated from the 1936 edition of *Innen Land: Ein Wegweiser in die Seele der Bibel und in den Kampf um die Wirklichkeit* (Buchverlag des Almbruderhof e. V.). This edition is based on the 1975 English edition translated by Winifred Hildel and Miriam Potts.

Cover image: *Desert in Color* (oil on canvas) by Erin Hanson, copyright © Erin Hanson. Used with permission.

A catalog record for this book is available from the British Library. Library of Congress Cataloging-in-Publication Data

Names: Arnold, Eberhard, 1883-1935, author.
Title: The conscience / Eberhard Arnold.
Other titles: Innenland. Volume 2, Kampf des Gewissens. English
Description: Walden, New York, USA : Plough Publishing House, [2019]
Identifiers: LCCN 2019021364 (print) | LCCN 2019980768 (ebook) | ISBN
   9780874862478 (hardback) | ISBN 9780874862485 (ebook)
Subjects: LCSH: Conscience--Religious aspects--Bruderhof Communities. |
   Bruderhof Communities--Doctrines.
Classification: LCC BJ1278.C66 A7613 2019 (print) | LCC BJ1278.C66
   (ebook) | DDC 248.4/897--dc23
LC record available at https://lccn.loc.gov/2019021364
LC ebook record available at https://lccn.loc.gov/2019980768

Printed in the United States

Dedicated to my faithful wife,
Emmy Arnold

Contents

Preface   *ix*

The Conscience and Its Witness   1

The Conscience and Its Restoration   33

Preface

Born to an academic family in the Prussian city of
Königsberg, Eberhard Arnold (1883–1935) received a
doctorate in philosophy and became a sought-after
writer and speaker in Germany. Yet like thousands
of other young Europeans in the turbulent years
following World War I, he and his wife, Emmy,
were disillusioned by the failure of the establish-
ment – especially the churches – to provide answers to
the problems facing society.

In 1920, out of a desire to put into practice the
teachings of Jesus, the Arnolds turned their backs
on the privileges of middle-class life in Berlin and
moved to the village of Sannerz with their five young
children. There, with a handful of others, they started
an intentional community on the basis of the Sermon
on the Mount, drawing inspiration from the early
Christians and the sixteenth-century Anabaptists.
The community, which supported itself by agricul-
ture and publishing, attracted thousands of visitors
and eventually grew into the international movement
known as the Bruderhof.

Eberhard Arnold's magnum opus, *Inner Land* absorbed his energies off and on for most of his adult life. Begun in the months before World War I, the first version of the book was published in 1914 as a patriotic pamphlet for German soldiers titled *War: A Call to Inwardness.* The first version to carry the title *Inner Land* appeared after the war in 1918; Arnold had extensively revised the text in light of his embrace of Christian pacifism. In 1932 Arnold began a new edit, reflecting the influence of religious socialism and his immersion in the writings of the sixteenth-century Radical Reformation, as well as his experiences living in the Sannerz community. Arnold continued to rework the book during the following three years, as he and the community became targets of increasing harassment as opponents of Nazism. The final text, on which this translation is based, was published in 1936. Arnold had died one year earlier as the result of a failed surgery.

This final version of *Inner Land* was not explicitly critical of the Nazi regime. Instead, it attacked the spirits that fed German society's support for Nazism: racism and bigotry, nationalistic fervor, hatred of political enemies, a desire for vengeance, and greed. At the same time, Arnold was not afraid to critique the evils of Bolshevism.

The chapter "Light and Fire," in particular, was a deliberate public statement at a decisive moment in Germany's history. Eberhard Arnold sent Hitler a copy on November 9, 1933. A week later the Gestapo raided the community and ransacked the author's study. After the raid, Eberhard Arnold had two Bruderhof members pack the already printed signatures of *Inner Land* in watertight metal boxes and bury them at night on the hill behind the community for safekeeping. They later dug up *Inner Land* and smuggled it out of the country, publishing it in Lichtenstein after Eberhard Arnold's death. Emmy Arnold later fulfilled her husband's wish and added marginal Bible references. (Footnotes are added by the editors.)

At first glance, the focus of *Inner Land* seems to be the cultivation of the spiritual life. This would be misleading. Eberhard Arnold writes:

> These are times of distress; they do not allow us to retreat just because we are willfully blind to the overwhelming urgency of the tasks that press upon human society. We cannot look for inner detachment in an inner and outer isolation. . . . The only thing that could justify withdrawing into the inner self to escape today's confusing, hectic whirl would be that fruitfulness is enriched by it. It is a question of gaining within, through unity with the eternal powers, that strength of character which is ready to be tested in the stream of the world.

Inner Land, then, calls us not to passivity, but to action. It invites us to discover the abundance of a life lived for God. It opens our eyes to the possibilities of that "inner land of the invisible" where "our spirit can find the roots of its strength." Only there, says Eberhard Arnold, will we find the clarity of vision we need to win the daily battle that is life.

The Editors

The Conscience and Its Witness

The conscience is an instinct to protect life
Life resists everything that would destroy it or kill
it. Life tries to build up its strength. It protects itself
instinctively against all the influences of death and
everything that is hostile and harmful. It is only
in a life that is going to rack and ruin – in one that
has already come under the power of death – that
the instincts fail and allow poisons to come in and
destroy life. Every organism endowed with a soul tries
as a united whole to ward off what is harmful to body
and soul.

The innermost part of the soul – the spirit – also
has an instinct for life. This is the conscience, which
as a first sign of inner life has become a watchman at
the threshold. It is the quiet, impersonal confidant
of the human spirit. "For no one knows what is in a
man except the spirit of the man, which is in him." 1 Cor. 2:11
The conscience is one of the most primeval stirrings
of life in the spirit. The spirit, as the profoundest part
of our being, has to represent our innermost calling.

The most necessary tool for this is the conscience, an instrument that warns, rouses, and commands.

The conscience is the spirit's sensitive organ of response. It has the task of warning the character against degeneration and destruction, because the character is meant to preserve moral order. The conscience has to show the character where it can find healing, strengthening, and the direction in life that it is meant to take. Every time the soul is deeply wounded, the conscience makes us painfully aware of it. It is a warning bell that sounds every time the spiritual life falls sick. Above all, it gives warning of the deadly misery of isolation, when the soul has separated itself from the core of life, from the destiny of its being – when it has separated itself from God. Therefore with all the urgency of love, it demands reconciliation with God and, with that, a uniting with all people. For unity is the hallmark of life. Unity finds fulfillment in God and his kingdom.

2 Cor. 5:18–21

The conscience leads to community

The conscience arouses in the individual conscious- ness a longing to come out of all constraint and isolation and to have community with the highest consciousness, the all-embracing consciousness of God. The result will be a unanimous accord and unity of life with all people who believe in God. This urge toward God and his community of life and faith accords with the nature of the human spirit as it was originally. Leibnitz describes God as the only object directly perceived by the soul that can be distinguished from the soul itself.[1] God is in direct

---

1 Gottfried Wilhelm von Leibnitz, 1646–1716, *Théodicée.*

contact with the soul and demands absolute love and community.

The conscience is the awakening of a direct consciousness of good and evil – a knowledge of what promotes life and what destroys it. As such, it can never be separated from the spirit's direct consciousness of God. It plays a part whenever the certainty of an absolute "thou shalt" or "thou shalt not" penetrates the consciousness. In the absoluteness of "thou shalt," God works directly on us. The urge of the conscience is to stand by our consciousness of God by demanding obedience to God. With every warning it gives, the conscience tries to help our consciousness of God on toward the free and willing obedience of faith.

Gen. 3:22

God wants to determine our life and lay obligations upon it through the conscience. Our consciences have been compared to mountains among which God's thunder echoes a millionfold. The further away the receiving heart is from the one who calls, the weaker will be the echo. The nearer we are when we receive the call of God, the more powerfully will our conscience be struck and impressed. There is always, however, a necessary distance between God's truth and our response. The conscience drives the anxious, hesitating heart nearer and nearer to the thunderous judgment over evil and to the revelation of good, lit up by the lightning. And yet it keeps us at a respectful distance. There will be no echo if there is no distance at all from the mountain wall.

"No one is good," Jesus tells us, "save God alone!" Whoever blasphemously identifies himself with God cannot hear the voice of God. If in our souls there is something of the breath of this one and only, who

Luke 18:19

Gen. 3:22–24

alone is good, then even in depraved and irreverent souls there will be a live witness. This witness will demand a distance and yet press closer because it judges evil and urges toward the good. It is the conscience of the human spirit. When we do evil, it warns and insists; it smites and punishes. It makes clear to us how far we are from God. But it does still more. Even though there is nothing good about us, this witness lives in our souls to make it possible for us to recognize good as good, to assure us that God is the only source of good, and to urge us on toward this source.

Even where consciousness of guilt seems to have died out, people cannot feel at home in their selfish existence. They are well aware that they lack inner unity and the community that takes shape as a result of it. Even the hardest heart yearns for this. We were created for community. Our conscience fights against things being turned so upside down that life is destroyed by selfish isolation. The conscience protests against every attempt to sever the living cohesion of things. Whenever a thread of life is broken, the conscience shows that it is wounded. Every time a person's inner being is divided and, just as much, every time the community that must come to outward expression is disrupted, the conscience gives a warning that life is being threatened by destruction. The conscience feels any disharmony as something terrifying and deadly because the very nature of the soul demands unity of life.

Any separation from God inevitably leads the human spirit to a deadly division within itself and to cold estrangement from others. When the conscience makes us aware of the urge toward God that is hidden

within us, a conflict arises between the true calling of
the ego and its actual condition. Every time we resist
this urge and act against it, our conscience blames no
one but us.

Julius Müller calls the conscience, even when it is
utterly ruined, the divine bond that ties the created
spirit to its origin.[2] That we belong to the people
of God, although we are degenerate and depraved
members, becomes clear in the conscience. It is the
longing for God that rouses opposition to evil. This
longing is for community in his kingdom of active
love, brought about by him alone. It opposes the
divisive power of the kingdom of mammon with its
lies, murder, and impurity. The conscience makes us
think about ourselves and our depraved condition
and, at the same time, about the revelation of the
higher truth of our original nature, our true nature.
It shows at the same time both our wretchedness and
our greatness.

The conscience is an inextinguishable part of
human consciousness. As such, it gives the strongest
witness that the origin of the human spirit is noble
and divine. The conscience never lets us quite forget
that this noble race has been called to be an image
of God however weather-beaten its coat of arms,
however deeply cracked, however overgrown with
moss. Even in the most erring offspring of the human
race, the memory of this image is never so irretriev-
ably lost that it cannot, through God's intervention,
be brought back to the light once more.

For this reason Paul, the apostle of Jesus Christ,
testifies expressly that even peoples estranged from

Eph. 2:10

Gen. 1:27

---

2 Julius Müller, 1801–1878, *Die christliche Lehre von der Sünde.*

God have a conscience. Paul is so deeply convinced of the divine origin of all living souls that he sees the Rom. 2:15 works of the Law written in the hearts of the heathen. In everything they experience and undertake, their consciences also give witness through the conflicting thoughts that accuse and excuse them.

After all, the living book of God's creation lies open for all to see; it points constantly to the divine Wisd. of Sol. 13:5, 7 calling for which man was placed in nature. Nature is a continual admonition to humankind, for nowhere has God's creation departed so far from its origin and Rom. 1:20 primeval purpose as in humanity. This is proved by the history of the human conscience.

Without God, the law dictates the conscience

Human beings were called to God's love. But when they so soon became murderous and would not let Rom. 3:10–12 themselves be judged and ruled by God's Spirit, the Gen. 6:3–13 pure, free Spirit gave up pleading with them. It no longer wanted to plead with them. Violence goes together with a lack of freedom. Therefore God sent them the law and conceded them the death penalty, at first in the form of the appointed blood-for-blood Exod. 21:24 revenge: an eye for an eye, a tooth for a tooth! "Whoever sheds the blood of man, by man again shall Gen. 9:6 his blood be shed."

Again, the servile spirit of the people who were meant to be God's people wanted a human king instead of God's rulership, instead of his dominion. God in his wrath had to give them a completely human authority to enforce severe punishment for 1 Sam. 8 murder and all wickedness. People today have long since forgotten what they have lost through these historical facts. Yet these measures to check still worse forces of evil must be recognized as necessary as long as people do not want to let God's spirit judge and rule.

The inner acquiescence given by the conscience can be seen in people's attitude to legal authority. For the sake of the conscience, it is still necessary for everyone to be subject to legal authority as the appointed servant of God. For this authority judges and punishes evil as the conscience demands. Yet as soon as the conscience is roused through God's spirit, it demands – even in the face of authority – that we should obey God rather than men, for God's kingdom demands recognition over and above all the kingdoms of this world. However, the prerequisite for this all-inclusive demand of God and his Spirit is fulfilled only when this Spirit who rules in God's kingdom really and truly rules over us, when he can actually plead with us and determine our whole life in an objective way according to God's kingdom.

Rom. 13:1–7

Acts 5:29–32

Through the judgment and power of governmental authority, the conscience is punished and sharpened. Through God's kingdom and his Spirit, it is set free and fulfilled. It seeks everywhere the source of the guilt that separates us from the rulership of God. In everything, the conscience wants to become clear in its judgment over the boundary between good and evil, because evil has separated us from God. Evil is its enemy. The conscience sees this enemy everywhere – waiting to the right and to the left, besetting us behind and before. Its most dangerous outpost of all is in our heart. The evil that surrounds and pervades our life is more than *our* enemy. It is *God's* enemy.

Rom. 8:2

Murder, lying, impurity, and property – this is the nature of evil. Jesus called the evil spirit "the murderer from the beginning" and "the father of lies," and called its subordinates impure spirits. Finally, he has confronted us with a decision: "You cannot serve God and mammon." God's rule is incompatible with killing, lying, sexual immorality, and, most of all, with the rule of property. Therefore God's kingdom is diametrically opposed to the evil powers of death and sin. This is true not only for the personal life of each individual but also for all powers of human authority, which want to fight evil and yet are rooted in the mammon of property: they cannot cut themselves loose from lying and impurity – they are driven even to mass murder.

John 8:44
Mark 1:23
Matt. 6:24
Luke 12:32–34

Detecting the enemy, however, achieves nothing more than reconnaissance before a battle. Even progress in the battle, even the annihilation of the enemy, does not signify that the victory is consummated. Only positive reconstruction gives triumph its value. Therefore the conscience longs for vigorous work at what is truly good in order to be able to celebrate the victory over evil.

When God rules, the conscience brings joy

The life of Jesus had nothing to do with killing and harming others, it had nothing to do with untruthfulness and impurity, and it had nothing to do with any influence of mammon or property. Jesus went even further: he smote this hostile power in its home territory. His death shattered every weapon of the enemy. But he did still more. He brought the kingdom of God down to the earth, he roused body and soul

Heb. 2:14–15
Mark 1:15

from death, he himself rose as the Living One, and through his Spirit he laid the foundation for the final kingdom – a kingdom of complete unity for everything in heaven and on earth. He broke down the barriers between nations, and he created the unity of the body of his church as his second incarnation. This new unity and bodily reality of Jesus lives here on the earth in the human race.

Eph. 2:14–22

We are called to this way as soon as we accept Christ's call. When through Christ and the Spirit we believe in the unity of God as the one and only good, when we live in faith through his strength, we lay aside everything that is opposed to perfect love. We fight it to the death on every front. We live as believers in the church of full community and are ambassadors of God's kingdom, representing Jesus Christ and commissioned by him. In this fight for the recognition of God's kingdom, in representing the final kingdom in opposition to all governmental authorities and powers of the kingdoms of this age, the conscience is the quiet ally of the Holy Spirit.

Eph. 4:15–32

Rom. 9:1

The conscience is that faculty of sensitivity in our inner being which responds with pleasure to every good deed and with displeasure to every evil deed. It exposes evil as alien and hostile to our nature as it originally was and as it is finally meant to be. Therefore, no supposedly superior point of view and no knowledge that sets itself up as progressive can ever reconcile the conscience to evil. As soon as God's Spirit takes possession of the human spirit to make a common witness, the conscience develops a most resolute firmness. It revolts with a revulsion that becomes almost unbearable every time love is

Rom. 8:16

wounded, every time love's obligations are neglected, every time love's justice is clouded, every time love's truth is betrayed, and every time God's kingdom is misrepresented.

Whenever human self-preservation seeks an advantage, a pleasure, or an influence that is contrary to the pure, absolute, and all-embracing love of Jesus Christ, the conscience – being now an instrument of the Holy Spirit – raises its voice in sharp protest in the name of the sovereign God and his absolute rule. With just as much intensity, it joyfully furthers every fulfillment of justice and social obligation, every unselfish act of devoted love, and every brotherly uniting in full community.

Eph. 6:10–17

The impulse of joyful agreement and inner satisfaction in our conscience when we have acted rightly in the works of love (at least as far as motive and aim are concerned) implies an assessment of values. In the same way, when evil and godlessness gain the upper hand in our life, the conscience experiences terrifying qualms of shame, disquiet, and silent self-accusation. These challenge us to evaluate our own actions. The conscience is constantly at work evaluating and passing judgment. It evaluates by feeling. It feels joy in what is good, for what is good is also just. It has joy in love, for love is also pure and genuine unity and community. It feels pain and revulsion against evil, for evil is also injustice. It feels pain about everything that is against love: that is, everything that destroys community, everything that is selfish, impure, hypocritical, and false.

The conscience wants to be the divine voice within us. It strives to show us what we are like (although we should be different), what we are not like (although we ought to know how we should be), what human society is like without community, and what the nations are like without the unity of the kingdom of God. The more the heart is touched by God's nature and his holiness, the more clearly does the conscience that is bound to Christ say what the church of God is, and the more clearly does it also show how, from the basis of the church, the believer should represent absolute love in a unity that brings peace and in a justice that results in community.

When we examine ourselves in the light of the destiny that God ordained for us, we become aware of the sharp contrast between what we should be and what we are. The conscience belongs to human consciousness and yet represents a "thou shalt" that is quite different from what humans are. The conscience is a decidedly subjective feeling, but it is based on and aims at an absolutely objective "thou shalt." Only when the demands of the conscience agree with the objective "thou shalt" do subjective impressions gain weight and meaning.

The unredeemed conscience torments
The conscience must represent an objective power that wants to take possession of us from within. It needs the Holy Spirit because within itself it does not have the power to rise above all that we are subjectively capable of. Without God's Spirit it is unable to represent clearly the cause it wants to serve. Yet even in remotest paganism, the conscience is active – although, without the Spirit of the cause, its accusations and demands are distinguished more by

unbridled ferocity than by shining clarity. Like the Furies in paganism, it pursues those who flee and seizes those who resist, so that even such masters of evil as the emperor Nero must undergo tortures of conscience.[3]

The comparison of the conscience with the Furies, those relentless spirits of doom and vengeance in ancient mythology, is all the more apt because the Furies serve just as much to protect the good and pure as to avenge crime. They cannot point anywhere to God's rulership because they know nothing of his Holy Spirit. They represent the conscience that is not yet illuminated by Christ, that does indeed know of good and evil but misses the way to the goal. They are handmaids of the holy order of natural life. They strive to represent that order of creation without which the life that lives and moves in a person's blood goes to its own destruction.

As might be expected, the Furies appear as daughters of night and death. They were brought into existence by the first crime that shed blood and destroyed a human life. Now, as pitiless goddesses who bring curses and wrath upon men to all eternity, they pursue to death everyone who commits a crime against the blood of life. Thus they chase the man who killed his mother. They are a dreadful picture of the bad conscience of the old nature with their horrible, gloomy figures, demonic snake hair, and torches brandished aloft.

The Furies are keen-sighted huntresses armed with whips and spears or bows and arrows. Shrouded in

---

3 Reference to the Erinyes of Greek mythology, called the Furies by the Romans. In Aeschylus's *Eumenides*, they chase Orestes, who has killed his mother to avenge the murder of his father, Agamemnon.

mist, they lie in wait for the evildoer, ready to distract his senses, derange his spirit, and suck his blood. For they too represent the old order: "blood for blood." Thus they correspond to the merciless authority of the criminal court, about which God spoke his awful word after the flood, when his Spirit no longer wanted to plead with perverse men: "I will demand your lifeblood. . . . Whoever sheds the blood of man, by man shall his blood be shed; for God made man in his own image." Gen. 9:5–6

Throughout all ages, sin against the blood of a soul endowed with the breath of God has struck the human conscience as the gravest crime, the capital offense against God and his order. Therefore, avenging it is seen as the first duty of human authority. The avenging authority (representing human order) and also the wild raging of the Furies (representing the unredeemed conscience) are far removed from the Spirit of the heart of God, and nothing can be found in them that reveals anything of the gospel of Jesus Christ. Yet hidden within them lies a corrective justice, a justice of wrath. It is the wrath of God, which through his judgment wants to make us ready for the perfect justice of love.

In this way the old Furies, as handmaids of punitive justice and as executioners of necessary law, are the strictest avengers of evil. But they are more. Like the authority of the state, they are intended to uphold and protect upright and repentant hearts. They hold their threatening snakebites in readiness for evildoers, but those who are good they greet with friendly eyes, bestowing their blessings as goddesses of the earth.

The Furies are more tormenting than any judicial authorities can ever be. For they are an objective personification of the conscience that has not yet been gripped by the gospel of perfect love. They symbolize the same punishment of conscience that Pestalozzi described so vividly centuries later.[4] When his character Hans Wüst rolls on the floor in torment over his perjury, howling like a dog whose entrails are torn, and when he tears his hair out and draws his own blood with his fists, the cry is wrung out of him: "Satan, cursed Satan, has me in his clutches!" Abuse, shame, and imprisonment are nothing to him compared with the horror, the despair, and the fear that God might never be merciful to him again. Here, in the eyes of the modern world, we see the Furies come to life again as agony of conscience.

The conscience calls to repentance

The same agony of conscience made Martin Luther cry out, "Oh, my sins, my sins, my sins!" He said about this indescribable torture:

> I know a man who declares he has often suffered this punishment. True, it did not last long, but it was so severe and so hellish that no tongue can tell of its severity, no pen can describe it, nor can anyone believe it who has not experienced it. It was such that if it had reached its peak or continued for half an hour longer – even a few minutes longer – he would have been utterly destroyed and all his bones burned to ashes. Here God appears, mighty in his wrath, and all creation too, so that a man knows not where to turn. There is no comfort, either from within or from without, and everything is full of accusations.[5]

---

4 Johann Heinrich Pestalozzi, 1746–1827, *Lienhard und Gertrud*.

5 Martin Luther, 1483–1546, *Erklärung und Beweis der Thesen*, 1518.

Luther's conscience at that time still stood in the midst of this deadly fear of wrath and punishment, outside the gate and outside the grace of God, and yet it pursued the positive goal of divine justice. The conscience is more than a protection for what is good, which has to be guarded from evil. It is more than the terrifying discovery that there is nothing really good in us. It is more than the punishment of evil through the justice of God. Rather, through devastating judgment of evil, the conscience must prepare the inner vision for the restoration of what is good. When the conscience is gripped and illuminated by the Spirit of God, it must prepare the way for faith and rebirth through deep repentance and a complete change of heart. The darkened inner eye must become like the sun so that it can see the kingdom of God. The conscience that is breaking down under wrath must be led to justice – to that justice which makes it possible for a new life of active love to arise out of faith.

Matt. 6:22

1 Tim. 1:5

The conscience, as a stirring of the human spirit, can never of its own accord reveal the kingdom of God. It can only strengthen the echo when the call to repentance reaches the heart – a call from God that pierces the heart and directs it to the kingdom of God. The call to life can only come from the origin of life, from God's heart. God's heart revealed itself in the voices of his prophets. In Jesus Christ it reached humankind as fullness of deity, as grace, and as truth. God created the conscience to be part of the life of the human soul, but it can do no more than answer his call as a call from the Holy Spirit. What it can do from its seat in the human spirit is to accept, affirm, and represent the demands made by God, that is, by the divine life of Jesus.

Col. 2:9

John 1:14–17

The conscience is nothing more than a human instinct for life. But it is able to expose and pursue everything that is hostile to the life that God alone is able to give. It is nothing more than a human instinct that is meant to point out and affirm everything that furthers and strengthens the life that God alone gives. Above all, as a moral conscience, it instinctively takes a stand against everything that opposes divine life, and consequently it supports all that is done out of diligence and enthusiasm for life. It lives for the love that springs into action through faith.

The conscience demands justice

The will of the divine Spirit strives to penetrate and rule over all areas of life. Consequently, the conscience that is awakened by the Spirit cannot be restricted by any narrowing of the moral will. Even the highest code of ethics cannot exhaust the depths of the conscience. We can merely hint at the fact that the conscience embraces all areas of life. As the aesthetic conscience, it promotes joy in what is beautiful, elevating, and pure. From deep within, it cleanses our taste – also in how we fashion things – from filth and ugliness and from all artificiality and insincerity. As an intellectual conscience, it is the instinct for intellectual integrity; it has an understanding for what must be acknowledged as true and expresses it in accordance with the facts. As a social conscience, it demands the dedication of the whole of our life, with all our strength and all our possessions, to the service of love – to brotherliness, to justice, and to full community with the poor and oppressed. As a religious conscience, it wants all this for the sake of God's truth, for his love and justice – that is, for

the supreme demand of unity with God himself and
unity with his absolute sovereignty. Everywhere,
the conscience is revealed as the heart's subjective
will for truth, for justice, and for unity. In all things,
it demands obedience in the face of the objective
absolute. The absolute will of God challenges the
conscience to let him become acknowledged Lord
over everything on earth.

Jesus Christ proclaimed, in accord with the divine
word of the Jewish prophets, that the will of God's
love is turned toward the earth and its peoples. He
alone has brought the authority and reality of his
kingdom to the earth and to humankind. The social
will toward brotherly justice and the active will
toward peace (born of love for our enemies) are possible nowhere but on the ground of Christianity or
under its influence and direction. This is why some
individualistic anarchists have called communism
and atheistic socialism a secularized expression of
Christianity. And indeed, this phenomenon in Europe
would never have been possible without Christianity's
love for one's neighbor, its equality of birth, its faith
in the future as faith in the kingdom of God, and its
social conscience awake to God's will.

When the conscience has found God's justice in
Christ, it recognizes human injustice as the opposite
of his love and of his aliveness. God's justice, which
comes to expression in Jesus, is greater than the
justice of the state with its legal rights and courts,
greater than the religious and social justice of theolo-
gians and moralists. Like salt, like a light, like a tree,
it is a real and living power of radiant warmth, strong
support, and protection – the real power of life in all
its fullness. Therefore the life that God's justice gives

Mic. 6:8

Rom. 13:8–10
Gal. 5:14

Matt. 5:20
Matt. 5:13–16
Ps. 1

Ps. 92:13–15

birth to as perfect love must be completely different from the life born of any other justice, however socially minded.

Even the social conscience of the believer does not exhaust the truth of this life (although this truth remains the most important expression of the social conscience among people). Christianity has shown that honesty toward oneself is the basic prerequisite for a Christian life. Even its bitterest opponents have to admit that the intellectual history of Christianity has produced an increasing exactness in the conception of truth. They can see that the sensitivity of the Christian conscience has been transferred to the scientific conscience, producing the finest intellectual integrity. The continual sharpening of the instinct of truthfulness has meant such a growth in scholarly exactness that Friedrich Nietzsche had to admit: "Conscientiousness in small things – the self-control of the religious person – was a preparatory school for the scientific or scholarly character and, above all, for the attitude in which we can treat a problem seriously without taking into consideration how it affects us personally."[6] Nietzsche himself recognized that when scientific positivism makes an idol of lifeless knowledge, it does not do justice to life.

The intellectual conscience of the believer also does not exhaust the truth of life. The conscience that follows Christ recognizes that what is untrue is the opposite of what is alive and essential to life. Truth means more than the intellect being indisputably right. Truth must seize the ultimate reality of life

Matt. 5:37

---

6 Friedrich Wilhelm Nietzsche, 1844–1900, *Der Wille zur Macht.* Arnold wrote his doctoral thesis on Nietzsche and Christianity.

in all that is genuine and essential to life, in all that
is unadulterated and clear, in all that has effective
strength and power. Consequently truth, in unity
with justice, must show itself as the very marrow of
life, as vital energy and courage, as a productive joy in
creative work, and as the power of love. Truth, as love,
is master of the essential nature of things.

The activity of the conscience is not limited to the
condemnation of what is evil, unlovely, and wrong. It
works toward the acceptance of all the life-energies
of love, for they are the very core of life. Just as love
itself never ends, so the conscience that works for
love can never come to the end of its activity. The
conscience can never put a stop to its working. Even
though it may not always have to suffer to the same
degree from the consciousness of what is evil, ugly,
and untrue, and even if there were nothing good that
needed its protection, the work of the conscience
would never come to an end.

A good conscience is more than just a conscience
that is not bad. It is not only a witness that condemns
or approves but, above all else, it is a voice that
impels us to loving dedication. This is true even with
pagan peoples when, imperfect as their community
may be, they want to act according to the law of the
community imprinted on their hearts. We can see it
perfected in Paul, the apostle of Jesus Christ, when
his heart beat truly for his people and demanded   Rom. 12:1
a readiness for the ultimate sacrifice. A good
conscience never waits in passive silence; it always
longs for and drives toward action. It impels the will
toward a truly loving life and, ultimately, toward God
and his kingdom.

On its own, the conscience is unreliable

Something of the demands made by this active conscience can be traced in all pagan peoples. Four centuries before Christ, Socrates was not only saved from making false steps by his inner voice, but he was also driven to constructive action. Above all, he was led to the choice of his higher vocation – the search for truth through inquiry and discussion with all and sundry. Yet his inner voice was nothing but the instinct of his soul, as unclear as it was strong, and just this inner voice gives proof that the human conscience, when it is not renewed by God's Holy Spirit, remains clouded in confusion in spite of the most strenuous efforts to find the truth. The fact that Socrates called this inner voice a demon points (rather like the Furies) much more to the dark rays of the other world than to the bright revelation of truth in the pure and perfect love of God's righteousness. It is dangerous and misleading to think, as many do, with the great Christian poet Dante: "A conscience stands beside me, pure and true, an authority in whom I trust completely and without reserve."7

Heb. 9:14

To regard one's conscience as an infallible authority is rash, to say the least. In and of itself, it cannot ever become pure and incorruptible because it continues to have a part in every degradation of the soul. It is rather like a ship's pilot who has lost his bearings because he has sailed into unfamiliar waters. Whether he admits his own helplessness with honesty and shame or whether he steers the ship this way and that with apparent confidence, he cannot do what he is meant to do until he has found his way

7 Dante Alighieri, 1265–1321, *The Divine Comedy: Inferno*, XXVIII.

back to his own familiar waters. The conscience
would indeed always like to steer the right course. But
it has lost its way. It longs for the home port, but thick
fog has clouded its vision. The land has disappeared
into the distance as if forever – the land of clarity. The
conscience asks the same alarmed question again and
again: "My poor, erring soul, will you ever find the
way home? How far will you have to go before you see
a light?"[8]

But just when the danger becomes obvious – when
immediate disaster threatens because the head is
perplexed and the heart grows faint; when visibility
is poor and destructive icebergs or rocks loom ahead;
or when collision with others whose course is just as
erratic is imminent – just when there is utmost need,
the conscience becomes disquieted and is nearest
to fulfilling its task. Therefore a bad conscience – a
conscience full of sin, an evil conscience – is all that
many people are aware of. This fact remains, and it
must be recognized again and again in the midst of
all the confusion today: the witness of the conscience
shows itself most sharply of all in the face of guilt and
threatening destruction.

The heart is like a secret chamber of justice in
which the conscience, as the judge within, challenges all that takes place. A shadow of God's will
remains printed, as it were, in the heart, even if it is
only scarcely visible. The judge within has to pass
a verdict in accordance with these faint lines. He is
busy day and night. He seeks judgment and atonement uninterruptedly. And yet one thing is always
clear – the conscience does not give atonement. We

---

8 First lines of a poem by Gustav Falke, 1853–1916, "Meine arme, irrende
Seele, wirst du nach Hause finden?"

ourselves cannot still our conscience. Consequently, it testifies with unquestionable authority to God-fearing people of all ages that burnt offerings and sacrifices, sacrifice of things and even sacrifice of life, make no one perfect.

Heb. 9:9

Splendid ceremonies and symbols of the utmost devotion mean nothing to a tortured and burning conscience unless the source of its distress is removed. In spite of the most earnest piety or the most genuine idealism, the conscience never ceases to condemn sin in all its heaviness as sin, which we of ourselves can never expiate. Even if we sacrifice our very lives for our ideals, the conscience still speaks to us of sin whenever we do something in the course of our sacrifice that offends God's truth and purity, that is, his unity and love.

Heb. 10:1–2

It is only through the knowledge of good and evil that this unremitting accusation of sin could arise. This knowledge became part of the first man when he joined forces with sin. Previously, like a child today, he had no awareness of a conscience in this sense, that is, in the sense of a bad conscience. Like every true child, he knew nothing about evil. In his innocence he was unable to discriminate or choose between good and evil. For it is only possible to "discern" spiritual powers, good or evil, by becoming one with them in will and deed.

Gen. 3

It is true that the first man, like a child, knew that he had to do the will of God. Yet he knew as little as any child to what extent God's will stands in opposition to evil. Without a doubt, he had the deep urge, like every childlike soul, to do the will of him who gave him life and breath. This urge was in no way strengthened when the utterly new and completely

different knowledge of good and evil came to him as
a bad conscience about sin. It could only hinder and
paralyze this basic yearning of life.

Man became a coward and a weakling. His conscience realized the evil he had done, but he was held
captive and powerless. He still had a little will left,
but this will had become sick and paralyzed through
choosing evil. He could of himself no longer do good.   Rom. 7:18–24
His conscience recognized good, but it did not lead
him to God; on the contrary, it drove him to hide in   Gen. 3:8
shame and fear.

How could it be otherwise? A defiled conscience
does not have within it the power to purify itself. It
sees no way out of the derangement and confusion
into which the knowledge of evil has plunged it.
It cannot achieve its goal until rebellious man has
returned to the life that he has deserted – a life in
God. Man must serve God again with a free will and
a clear conscience. This freedom and purity are to
be found nowhere except in God. They are not to be
found among people.

In rebirth, the conscience finds its bearings
This return, therefore, means a complete turning
away from all that is purely human in the inner life.
It means a break with the whole structure of public
life as people have created it, a break with all existing
conditions, and that means a turning to the life of
Jesus and his coming kingdom. Only here can the   Mark 1:15
conscience be freed – released from its association
with evil. Only here can community with God be
found – a complete transformation of the inner and
outer life to correspond to the childlike spirit and the
origin of the first man.

Heb. 10:22

Rom. 2:4 God in his loving-kindness will do everything possible to move the heart to this conversion. In every event, whether in the history of the great world or in our own small world, God seeks through his loving-kindness – and through the wrath of his judgment – to lead us to radical repentance, a repentance John 3:5 that leads to rebirth and to the kingdom of God.

In the composure of prosperous middle-class life, we had hardened our hearts against this message from God. Consequently, the iron plow of bitter need had to tear open our consciences. Our consciences had to be awakened by need and distress so that they might again condemn all evil and search out all good, so that they might learn again to listen to the Word of truth and to establish God's future in the present.

Ultimately, the business of the conscience is to represent the truth. The nearer it comes to converting people and all that relates to them, the more it thirsts for the ultimate truth and the life that truth brings, a life that changes everything and makes everything possible. The conscience responds to the truth. The writings of the apostles and the prophets testify that every genuine proclamation of the Word, every unadulterated revelation of the truth, speaks to the Acts 23:1

Acts 24:14–16 conscience of all people. The conscience recognizes the objective truth of the Word and the subjective honesty of the confessor for what they are. Beck's saying, "Christianity looks to our consciences for authentication," refers first and foremost to the inner testimony to objective truth.[9] But this testimony also includes the authentication of all God-ordained proclaimers of the gospel as to the sincerity of their

---

9 Johann Tobias Beck, 1804–1878, *Outlines of Biblical Psychology.*

intentions and the harmony between their words and
their way of life. The Word brings truth and is truth. John 17:17
From those who proclaim it, the Word demands the
integrity and reality that befits the truth.

When God's message awakens us, it tries to strike
our consciences in such a way that we can never
seek or long for anything but what God is saying.
From now on, we seek the kingdom of God and his
righteousness. In all the things that are added to us
on earth, God's purpose is to give us the same task
as he gave to the first people: we are to cultivate and
preserve what God entrusts to us, and we are to penetrate it in spirit, designate it clearly, and proclaim it. Gen. 2:8–16
Our consciences must become free for this life task.

The church is to restore the lost garden

Just as God once gave the first man and woman the
peace and community of the old garden, he gives this Ps. 72:3, 7
task to the believer in the new garden of his peaceable Isa. 51:3
kingdom, which is the church community of the new Isa. 58:11
Spirit. It is for the task of cultivating the earth for his Ps. 85:8–14
rulership that he wants to purify the conscience from Ezek. 36:35
its self-willed and hostile separation. The curse of
this separation lies more obviously before the eyes of
people today than any other generation. God's garden
is more remote than ever before. The separation is
constantly increased by frenzied travel as we rush
with headlong speed over an earth deprived of God.
At the same time, though, God and his kingdom draw
near in secret to win back the garden, here where it
was lost.

The contrast between the kingdom of God and
the kingdom of mammon has seldom come so clearly

to light in the history of humankind as in our time. We are in a similar situation to that of Reformation times. At that time the reformer Jakob Hutter worked throughout all the German territories of Tirol and Moravia, from 1529 until his martyrdom in 1536. He proclaimed once again the entire gospel of God, founding and establishing for thousands the complete community of the united church based on faith in the kingdom of Jesus Christ. Among other important letters of the year 1535, he wrote the following one (delivered from Tirol to Moravia by Wolf Zimmermann), in which he testifies vividly to faith in the showers of living water from above – faith in the constructive and strengthening power of the Holy Spirit and the healing mercy in Jesus Christ:

> May God shower these blessings upon our hearts and bless his garden so that it may become fruitful with all good works. This garden is the church of the living God. May God fence this garden for you and make a wall around it, shield it, and protect it so that the fruit may ripen; for the Lord's pleasure-garden blossoms now! The children of the Lord thrive and grow in godly righteousness and truth like lilies and flowers, as a lovely garden flourishes after a gentle May shower. Yes, their hearts burn with the fire of God's love. Their hearts are alight and kindled by the eternal light and fire of God. Therefore they are justly called a pleasure-garden of the Lord and a paradise of God. The holy city cannot be hidden.[10]

The same divine community of peace and the same work of love for the earth are entrusted in our time

---

10 Jakob Hutter, *Brotherly Faithfulness: Epistles from a Time of Persecution* (Plough, 1979), Letter VI.

to this same church, this garden of God, as it was
once entrusted to the first man and woman. Into
the church's hands is entrusted the building up of
the same justice that will conquer the whole world
in the final kingdom of Jesus Christ. The lordship of
the Spirit over soul and body (and therefore over all
that belongs to the earth) shall be revealed once more
in the church as the image of God as it is given in
Jesus Christ. The gospel of God wants to awaken our
consciences for this task, given to the first man and
to the last Adam. We have to accept this task even
though we are not equal to it.

1 Cor. 15:45

The blood of Jesus purifies the conscience

Sickness of soul and spirit has eaten so deeply into
our conscience that it is no longer able to be a clear
mirror of good and evil. Least of all can it give a clear
picture of God's image. In spite of the testimony
it gives again and again, it is stained by evil in the
soul. Just as it is unable to keep itself from being
besmirched, the conscience is also unable to purify
itself. Of itself, it is not only incapable of producing a clear picture, it cannot even reflect in clear
outlines the radiant image of God that shines out so
wonderfully in Jesus. The conscience needs constant
purification.

The human conscience can be purified in no
other way than through the sacrificed lifeblood of
Jesus Christ, who was and is the only pure image of
God. His sacrificed soul brings God's life to us. To
have faith in our own blood – faith in the beauty of
the soul or the purity of the race – is to confuse and
pervert facts as they truly are. The blood of every one

Heb. 9:14

Rom. 5:12 of us proves to be burdened with an evil inheritance. It shows its own utter impurity. "The soul lies in

Lev. 17:11 the blood." Therefore, throughout the ages, all the weaknesses and failures of human life are revealed in the bloodline of the individual, of the nation, and of humankind. Faith in Jesus Christ holds firm to nobler blood. The soul of his blood was ruled and filled by the pure Spirit of God's love. No other human life can be compared with it. Therefore he is more than a

1 Cor. 15:45 living human soul. He is the quickening Spirit.

Jesus represents in his life the only human soul

1 Pet. 1:19 that kept free from all stain. The life of his soul, like ours, was in his blood. His blood and his body were also bound together in mutually dependent unity. But his body was without sin; his blood was pure; his conscience was undefiled. When he sacrificed his life for us, his blood was free from any guilt of his own. His blood was free from all impurity, all ungenuineness, and all covetous desires. It was free from every guilt, including the heaviest that can lie on human hands: that of shedding human blood. No matter what the circumstances or how lofty the ideals, Jesus had nothing to do with this gravest of crimes, the crime against life given by God alone, life that only God is entitled to take away. No war and no death sentence can be justified by appealing to him. He could commend his spirit into the hands of the Father free

Luke 23:46 from the stain of this guilt as of all guilt. His was a living spirit that had not been corrupted by anything belonging to death or leading to death.

From God he once more sends this quickening

John 14:26 Spirit down to us. Those who receive this pure Spirit will have their souls and consciences purified from

all former guilt, and their lives will be protected
from new offenses, for the life of Christ, the bearer
of this Spirit who was sacrificed for them, is purity
itself – the purity of a love that is perfect unto death.
The blood that was sacrificed for them in death is
mightier than death and more powerful than all its
deadly, poisonous, and divisive powers, for it bears
within it a life that has remained free from all the ele-
ments of death and decomposition, which are hostile
to life and to God. Purification through the blood of
Christ means that in his Spirit his spotless, surren-
dered life unfolds its powers here and now. Therefore,   1 Pet. 2:24–25
it is able to set our consciences free from all impurity.

Through the complete uniting of his life with ours,
his sacrifice has the power to purify our consciences
from all guilt and confusion. It gives our consciences   Heb. 10:19–22
the highest and purest of tasks, for his sacrifice
created unity: the new unity, and the only unity there
is among people. It created the organic unity of the
kingdom and the church, which does not tolerate a
single barrier between the nations. For it has broken
down the strongest barrier between peoples – the
barrier that stood between the Jewish people and
other nations. Whoever tries to erect this barrier   Eph. 2:13–22
again – or insists on the erection of other walls
between peoples – is a traitor to the blood of Christ
and his sacrifice. All that takes place as a result of this
attitude is bound to show itself as the work of death,
because it is inimical to the Spirit of Life. All works
that establish self-willed boundaries are and remain
dead works.

In spite of its profound weakness, the conscience
is in this respect true to the origin of the soul in God,

the source of life, in that it fights against all dead works. Through the blood of Christ, the conscience strives to do away with all works done in human strength. Such works can never create life anywhere, for they are undertaken without the Spirit of Christ and without the power of God. When works are born out of our own strength, arising from our own motives and pursuing our own aims, they are dead works. When they deny the origin of life and God's goal in Christ Jesus, they are dead works.

Purified consciences reflect God's image

The Gospels would have us rest from all our own works so that God's work can begin through his Spirit just as it did in the first church in Jerusalem. God begins his work now. The Holy Spirit establishes it. Jesus Christ accomplishes it. In God it is consummated. When the conscience is purified from all that belongs to evil and death, it sets to work harder than ever before. Now the mystery of faith has to be kept safe in a clear conscience. Now the new life has to set to work, as God's love and God's work, in deeds of love that are born of a pure heart, a good conscience, and a sincere faith.

Heb. 4:10

Acts 2–4

1 Tim. 1:5

The awakened conscience exerts its humble strength more and more so that all available means and gifts are used for the fulfilling of God's will – for the work that only God can do. Perfect love longs to express itself in God's work among all people so that each person is done justice and so that as many as possible reach an awareness and fulfillment of their highest destiny.

The conscience expects us to put into action the dignity we have rewon in God and to let it bear rich fruit. This new nobility bears the image of God on its coat of arms. It accepts responsibility for God's kingdom of justice in the joy of love and in the unity of peace. The conscience that is purified in Christ, as a conscience that is in the Holy Spirit, seeks the image of God. Only in the church of Christ and in the kingdom of God can it be established anew among us. The image of God appears wherever the Spirit of the church's Master is, the Spirit of the king of the kingdom. The features of God's character stand out more and more clearly, more and more radiantly. The conscience that has been illumined by the Spirit recognizes that it is our vocation to be the image of God. Once that has happened, the conscience has nothing to do with any other witness. It has become the finger in Grünewald's painting, pointing to the figure of the Crucified One.[11] The image of man, which has already been repainted a hundred times, has been renewed in the image of Jesus Christ and now appears once again as the image of God.

Gen. 1:27

Col. 3:10

Rom. 14:17

Eph. 4:24

2 Cor. 3:17–18

Rom. 9:1

1 Cor. 15:49

---

11 Reference to Matthias Grünewald's *Isenheim Altar* (ca. 1516), a triptych that portrays John the Baptist pointing to the crucified Jesus.

The Conscience
and Its Restoration

The conscience is a sensitive instrument
The conscience is an organ of extraordinary delicacy
and sensitivity, representing the deepest feelings of
the human spirit. It is like a supersensitive recording
instrument, influenced by every change of weather
and liable to be seriously damaged by any shock.
When life becomes more and more superficial,
when every door is thoughtlessly left open to the
atmosphere of the times with its changing winds
and temperatures, the conscience is in danger of
being thrown off balance. But not only then: it can
be led astray just as much by mental and intellectual
development. Even an increase of religious activity
can cause serious derangement. The conscience is an
uncertain factor even in the holiest spheres of life.

The conscience is diseased as long as it is not
healed by the power of Jesus' surrendered life. Bound
to false ideals, that is, to erroneous human thinking,
the conscience is unreliable and degenerate until it   1 Cor. 8:7, 12
experiences freedom – and asserts its freedom – in
the true and vital Word of God, in the living Spirit

of Jesus Christ. Only in doing the will of God is the
spirit given health. Jesus declared this with unmistakable authority; he put it into practice and sealed it
with his death. Any other idea, however strongly
represented, makes the conscience uncertain and
ineffective.

The conscience craves for the very essence of
truth. It demands an ultimate, indisputable goal.
Strength of conscience, a growing certainty and
clarity, is to be found only where peace rules as unity,
only where justice rules as brotherliness, only where
joy rules as pure and all-inclusive love. Every other
ideal, no matter how praiseworthy it may seem, has
disastrous and even fatal results if it aims at other
goals even for a short time. The one way that leads
upward has both solitary paths and wide, well-
traveled highways branching off it. Every one of them
leads us further and further away from unity, justice,
and love. They bring us into darkness, uncertainty,
and division. In the end, they plunge us into the
abyss. The conscience, as a faculty of weak humans, is
supersensitive and all too easily brought into danger
on false paths and then corrupted and destroyed.

The unhealthy state of an erring conscience comes
to expression in annihilating self-accusations and in
hateful reproaches so violent that they derange the
mind. Dissension and hate undermine the health and
vitality not only of individuals but also of nations.
Sickness shows itself most of all when the conscience
reacts in a very sensitive way in the wrong place. It
is typical of all false ideals and goals that they rob
the conscience of certainty about the essential thing.
They all bind the conscience to secondary issues.

Matt. 7:24–29

Matt. 7:13–14

Col. 2:16–19

They all serve dissension. They all shake trust in the Spirit who unites and purifies. This is because they all wish to set arbitrary boundaries to limit the cause they should be representing. On the one hand they blunt the conscience, and on the other hand they incite it to wild exaggeration and injustice.

1 Cor. 10:23–30

The conscience starts to go wrong when we lose trust in the uniqueness and absoluteness of the goal. In the end, confidence and clarity are given up as lost forever. As long as other points of attraction compete with the magnetic pole, the compass needle jerks unsteadily here and there without any accuracy. This restlessness gives rise to a wavering judgment which, like a bird of prey, looks for a victim. There are cases in which a sick conscience lets no thought arise and no step be taken without submitting it to serious misgivings and harsh judgments. Such a sickness fills the whole of life with grievances and dissatisfaction, with self-laceration and injustice.

Healing through remission of sin

Only when the conscience that inflicts such suffering on itself experiences the remission of sins through Christ can healing be given. When accusation comes to an end, impure fires are extinguished and their unsteady flickering dies out. As soon as the pure light of loving grace breaks through, hostility and injustice sink into ashes. The fire of evil dies away in God's air. Those who have been forgiven much love much. Those who experience love forgive much. When the power of all-embracing unity breaks through, division and destruction vanish, and all their misleading and subsidiary aims vanish with them.

Rom. 2:15–16

Luke 7:47

It has been proved by experience that when a man wants to become healthy again, he begins by speaking about his malady openly and without reserve. Recovery has already begun when he frankly exposes the accusations and inhibitions of his conscience, recognizes the power of his censured urges as a reality, brings to light the morbid repression of these urges, and makes known his self-laceration and hostility and all the injustice that goes along with them. To conceal these exhausting struggles is to sap the energy of life, as the Jewish Psalms testify with superlative clarity. By disentangling conflicting forces in a matter-of-fact way and exposing all the aims and motives behind them, anyone can knock the bottom out of this exhausting conflict.

Ps. 32:5

Yet here too, disclosing the harm is only the first step. The next important step will be to show the corrupted and repressed urges the way to healing and the sphere of action that God intends for them. The conscience must find God's land, in which joy in life – which is God's will – takes the place of the despondency and despair to which all human unrest is doomed.

Prov. 28:13

For this reason, any attempt at pastoral help is bound to be inadequate and futile as long as the conscience is not entirely freed from soul-killing accusations and self-accusations and from the sweat of its own desperate efforts. Nothing that is reaped from the accursed soil of our own efforts or self-appointed goals can stand before the conscience or before the final judgment seat. Our consciences must be freed from our own spirit, from our own will, our own goals, and our own works. All of life's energies must be directed toward the one and only task in life that is truly active and positive: carrying out God's creative will and working toward the goal of his new creation. Subconsciously, the conscience does have this one goal before it even when it is not clearly aware of all this because of its seriously sick and degenerate state.

Today's society despises the conscience

In times past, there was a tendency to call even the healthiest reactions of the conscience a sign of sickness that should be ignored. There is the same tendency again today in a new form. But it has to be repudiated most decisively. The conscience must never be silenced or despised. Rather, it must be led to splendid health by being freed from false aims and directed toward the kingdom of God. That never means that the conscience is silenced or despised - rather, it gains positive recognition through being filled with new clarity and new content. This freeing and fulfillment leads to lively activity in all areas of life embraced by the conscience. It is truest of all for public responsibility and vocational activity: in these areas, plain for everyone to see, completely new ways and unheard-of possibilities will be opened up by the conscience that is bound to Christ and his kingdom.

Heb. 13:18

The same is true for all areas of life: they are filled with new meaning and given new purpose. This includes being freed from property, bloodshed, and lying just as much as being purified in the area of sex. Human existence as a whole is at stake. It must be won completely or given up as lost. Many people are so bewildered by the utter confusion of life today that they cannot summon enough strength and clarity of conscience to have a decisive effect on even one area of their character. They are and continue to be at a loss.

During and after the [First] World War, all manner of dishonest business practices gained ground, even in circles that had long shown a certain sureness of moral instinct. In more than half the German nation, any effective defense the conscience might have had against the powers of hell had been destroyed – by political murder (lightly interpreted as self-defense) and by thoughtless readiness for a repetition of war and civil war.

Whoever can read the signs of the times will hardly be surprised to find that there is scarcely any real uneasiness about the injustice of mammon and property – an injustice that in fact kills every bit of love and the whole of life. In the obvious confusion of conscience among people, it is not surprising to find a lack of restraint over covetous desires and a brazen unfaithfulness that is growing beyond all bounds. The masses are in motion. The human race is gravitating around a turning point. In all probability this critical and turbulent state will lead to destruction. Ominous signs gather on all sides. The greatest danger in all the different areas that are corrupt today is this: spiritual leaders explain the ever-increasing confusion in such bedazzling ways that no one feels uneasy.

"Repression" can be healthy

Nowadays what is most abnormal has become the norm, or at least accepted as an ordinary necessity of

life by almost everyone. The present-day confusion
of conscience with regard to sex must be mentioned
here as a typical example, one that is characteristic of
all areas of life. In the circles influenced by Sigmund
Freud, people attempt to draw all kinds of sexual
perversions out of the slumbering subconscious
regardless of whether these are committed on one's
own body, on the opposite sex, or on the same
sex. They regret that these perversions have been
repressed into the subconscious by the conscience.

Followers of Freud probe into earliest childhood
and into the most spiritual relationships, trying to
prove that even such pure feelings as those between
parents and children are based on erotic drives that
determine our whole life. And what Freud himself saw
as a general principle applying to scientific research
has been used by some of his followers for practi-
cal orientation and guiding principles in personal
conduct. This is bound to have very harmful effects.

People try to bring into the clear light of consciousness images that can only be recognized as
morbid. They intentionally try to bring these images
back into channels from which they had been
diverted by a healthy reaction of the conscience. In   1 Cor. 4:4–5
all of this, there is a marked tendency to attribute
all emotional disturbances to repressed sexual
desires – desires that were actually hardly noticeable
or that were long since inwardly overcome. What
is most dangerous of all (and even seductive) is
that these impulses that have been driven into the
subconscious and forgotten there are supposed to
be cured by being brought back again as consciously
willed images. It amounts to an attack on the

conscience – an attack that distorts everything. It is impossible to imagine a worse attack or one that leads people further astray. The would-be cure leads to a sickness and poisoning that grows progressively more widespread and more serious.

And yet even these circles have had to admit that "culture" and "true humanity" are possible only through a repression of sexuality, which can never have a cramping effect when it takes place through the pure Spirit. Even these circles must recognize the repression of impulses by the conscience in the human soul as the necessary link between sexuality and spirit. Without this link, the spirit would be cut off from our life.

On the other hand, the deliberately chosen word "repression" is enough to deprecate the whole activity of the conscience and throw suspicion on it. It is wrongly understood, however: this dangerous word does not apply to a healthy conscience. Yet it is not without significance. There would indeed be a fatal repression, a morbid suppression of vital impulses, if the active conscience were not able to point to a responsible way in which all the powers of body and soul could be led to a positive and creative task.

Here lies the real reason why this dangerous misconception is so widespread in our sick age. In the concept of the family almost universally accepted today, the responsibilities and tasks of family life no longer correspond to God's creative will. What is true of parents is true of children. Countless young people, and just as much their parents, lack that sense of inner responsibility in their mutual relationships which puts the whole of life into the hands of God's faithful Spirit, who unites for eternity.

Large numbers of our contemporaries suffer no pangs of conscience when the soul's deepest need for faithfulness is destroyed. They are affected just as little when the smallest souls that want to be called into life are prevented or annihilated. Little souls wait in vain to be called out of eternity. Living human souls wait in vain to be called by constancy and faithfulness. There seems to be an ever smaller circle of people in whom the conscience protests clearly and sharply against contempt for the creative Spirit, just as it protests against any profanation of the longing for unity, faithfulness, and constancy.

This inner protest is also a stirring challenge to us to shape our love life responsibly and faithfully. Anyone wanting to call it "repression" casts suspicion on the very creation of man. In actual fact, this activity of the conscience provides us with our only safeguard against the fall that threatens us, a fall that would make us lower than the animals, lower than the beasts of prey. A comparison could be made with a war veteran who is emotionally disturbed, or with the morbid excitement leading up to a civil war: in both cases, the conscience has to repress the passions that urge people to shoot fellow human beings in the streets of their hometown. In the same way, it is a healthy sign when a person represses uncreative and life-thwarting urges toward his or her own body, toward someone of the same sex, or toward a life companion of the opposite sex. If in any one area of our life we are not given the opportunity for responsible and constructive action, then we should be thankful that "repression" – a term so often misused – has led to the complete forgetting and extinguishment of desires that are sterile or murderous.

The enlightened conscience will see to it that the sultry, natural urges of the unthinking subconscious mind are not allowed to influence the thoughts of the soul: it will condemn as irresponsible what these urges want to do. No one can regard a sense of responsibility as morbid suppression. Every clear spirit must feel that it is a sign of a healthy mind when the conscience wards off each degenerate impulse or sterile activity through feelings of dislike and embarrassment, shame and disgust, or horror and fear. A conscience that works in this direction is on its way to recovery; it helps us overcome everything that would destroy the holiest powers of life. It is a question of what these powers are meant for. In the conscience that is regaining health, the creative Spirit awakens an awareness that all life-energies are meant for great and noble tasks, tasks that we cannot allow to be hindered or desecrated. The "faunic" man[12] crushes underfoot all the powers of conscience that threaten him. Without any feeling of shame or disgust, he wants to become one with every orgasmic deity; he wants, undisturbed, to say to each passing moment of desire, "I am lust itself." His lust is devoid of spirit and meaning, for it is altogether lacking in purpose and moral content. Such a man is not a victor but a miserable slave to the lecherous god.

The pagan faun is a symbol of the violation of all noble-mindedness. It desecrates the human spirit, and it is the enemy of the divine Spirit. The creative Spirit does not in any way spurn the body or its

---

12 The "faunic man" (faunischer Mensch), a phrase used by Arnold's contemporary Hans Blüher to describe a sexually uninhibited person. Blüher called those who repress sexual urges the derogatory name Mucker, translated here as "prude."

psychophysical powers when it banishes to hell this soulless, grinning pagan god who threatens everything that is holy. The pagan god is dead, and all he can do is to embrace death.

To be sure, this pagan god is not the only enemy of the creative will for life. In his presence, the conscience is stifled; but also in the sanctimonious "Christian" prude who grumbles against God's will, the conscience is trained to a morbid aversion to life. Such would-be Christians want to reject all the urges of the living senses as alarming and embarrassing. They ought to call themselves Buddhist rather than Christian. Buddhism is the supreme representative of powers of dying, turned away from the life of the earth.

God's creative intent for sex is still good

The attitude of Christ is utterly different: his life and death remain devoted to the earth. His will is that God's kingdom comes on earth! It is important that the conscience be so restored to health that the natural urges go in the direction meant for them. Then they will unfold without further harm in a way that corresponds to the will of creation. This healing can take place only through faith in the coming kingdom: faith in a power that is present here and now. Weighty reasons can be brought forward to support the opinion that this healing has become an impossibility for people of today. For only in connection with an absolute transformation of the whole of public life can a development of vital powers take place in this one and only living direction. To many people, this seems an impossibility in our present times; it has become too remote for their small faith.

Matt. 6:10

Moral philosophers may demand that the sexual life be purified by insisting on purity before and during marriage. But even the best of them become insincere and unjust if they do not make clear the actual basis for the fulfillment of such high demands. Even destruction of the life that is waiting to come into being – a Massacre of the Innocents intensified a thousandfold today – remains unassailable without faith in the kingdom of God. The supposedly high culture of our days will continue to practice this massacre as long as social disorder and injustice prevail. Murder of the unborn cannot be overcome as long as private life and public life are allowed to maintain their status quo.

Whoever fights against self-centered acquisitiveness and against the deceit in unjust social distinctions must fight them in such a realistic way that he can demonstrate a different form of life as a possibility that actually exists. If he does not, he cannot demand purity in marriage or an end of murder either. Not even for families with the soundest morals can he wish the blessing of many children that corresponds to the creative powers of God's nature. Christian marriage cannot be demanded outside the whole context of life that is called the "kingdom of God" and the "church of Jesus Christ."

Marriage alone fulfills the demands of the sexual conscience. It is a fulfillment through the will to have children. It is a fulfillment in the picture it gives of Eph. 5 the unity of God with his people, as an example of the rule of the Spirit of Unity, and as a community of life and community of goods. It symbolizes the rule of the Spirit over body and soul. In all these ways, marriage is a picture of the church. The place for marriage is nowhere but in the church. These demands can be made of marriage only where the unity of the church, proceeding from the Spirit, creates community in material things through inspired and united work. Only in the church can these demands be fulfilled at the right time and given their true value.

The unity and purity in marriage as taught by Jesus and his apostles are unique. They have nothing to do with the old nature. They belong much more to the new church order, which as brotherly justice lets the Spirit of Love rule supreme. Unity and purity in marriage do not belong to unredeemed man. They can only be realized in the new church of the Spirit of Jesus Christ. They belong to the kingdom of God. They are symbol and sacrament of that kingdom.

The Gospels embrace all aspects of life

The conscience is destined to lead us to God's love and to the fruits of all the gifts of God's love. The call of God's love leads us to unity in the Spirit through the invasion of the Spirit into every area of life and his rulership there. God's will is that we put this love into practice with all the strength of our body, soul, and spirit. God is love. Those who abide in love abide in God, and God abides in them. A life lived in love is *John 15:4–10* lived in God. The Father of Jesus Christ bestows his love here on earth so that love shall reign supreme here – so that what love dictates shall be done in everything here on earth. Only in this way will God's name be hallowed.

God is unchangeable. His name is "I am that I am." *Exod. 3:14* His heart embraces everything and remains the same for everyone. It was revealed in Jesus Christ. Jesus

Christ is today and forever the same as he was in all his words and deeds. He is here and now the same as he will reveal himself to be in his kingdom. His words of love point to the same way for all things. What he said for the future members of his kingdom holds

Matt. 5–7 good for all his disciples at all times. Everything he said for his disciples' instruction belongs together, just as the sap belongs to the tree, the savor to the salt, and the flame to the candle.

For this reason, what Jesus said about marriage must not be isolated from any other saying in the Sermon on the Mount. In marriage, Jesus represented the will to love as the will to unity. But he represented it just as much in not having property, not bearing arms, not insisting on rights, being free from a judging spirit, being forgiving, and loving one's enemies. Poverty born of love is a protection from a bad conscience because it guards against injustice, as Jesus the son of Sirach says in the Book of Ecclesi-

Ecclus. 20:21 asticus. Perfect love strides on to voluntary poverty because it cannot keep for itself anything that a neighbor needs. Perfect love does away with weapons because it has given up self-preservation and has nothing to do with revenge. It remains steadfast and

1 Pet. 3:14 for conscience's sake bears evil and injustice. It keeps in mind the Sermon on the Mount and knows that this attitude is God's greatest gift because it reveals his heart. The love that conquers everything is revealed by a firmness that is not upheld by weapons.

Love gives up all possessions. Like the elders of the early church, those who guard the mystery of faith in a pure conscience remain free from involvement in any legal or hostile action. Christ's justice conducts

1 Cor. 6:1–11 no lawsuits. It does not carry on a middleman's

business or any business that is to the disadvantage of
another. It foregoes all its own advantage, it sacrifices
every privilege, and it never defends a right. Christ's
justice never sits on a jury, never deprives anyone
of freedom, and never passes a death sentence. It
knows no enemies and fights no one. It does not go
to war with any nation or kill any human being. And
yet when this justice is at work, it is justice in its
most active form, peace in its most energetic form,
and constructiveness in its most effective form. The
sum total of all we are commanded to do is to love:
to love with a pure heart, a clear conscience, and a   1 Tim. 1:5
genuine faith. In order for perfect love to flow freely,
Jesus showed the conscience the way of responsible
community in God. This is the essential nature of his
kingdom and his church.

The way of Jesus is love, agape. His love tolerates   1 Cor. 13
no unclarity. This kind of love is unique. It gives a
very definite direction. It is a way, and this way is very
clearly marked out. In the experience of God's love,
Jesus Christ leads us up to the purest and loftiest
peaks of willpower, clear recognition, and a strength
of heart that is joy. He does not do this for our sake.
He wants us to pass on the streams of this power of
love that is poured into our hearts. These streams are
meant to flood the earth. They are meant to conquer
the land. They are meant to reveal God's heart and
establish God's glory.

God's glory is his heart, and his heart is love. It
devotes itself to all people in the joy of giving. God's
glory is love. Love is his justice. When our seeking
for the kingdom of God and his justice is single
and undivided, such a love for all people is kindled
in us that everything we want for ourselves we

want for everyone. That is the only justice, the only righteousness, when we give our lives for love. The kingdom of God represents the highest goal of this pure and unadulterated love of the active Spirit. This love alone fulfills the longing of our conscience. All other objects of our thoughts and inclinations prove to be either weak representations of the pure service of God's kingdom or distorted caricatures of it, its hostile antithesis. Nothing is conceivable to the purified conscience without the thoughts of perfect love. Unity is its first and last thought.

Christ's rule sets the conscience free
From first to last, life is called to unity with God, expressed as the unity of the church, the unity created by his Spirit of Love. In this community of brotherly love, the conscience gains a strength that goes beyond the rejection of what is wicked and evil. It becomes the driving power behind joyful, constructive work. The conscience that is fettered to Christ is bound to the king and Lord of the coming order of God. Therefore, it demands and creates everywhere the one form of life that strives to correspond to the order of the kingdom of God down to the last detail. In Christ, we are concerned in all areas of life with the greatest and highest that can be entrusted to us: the eminence of God, the rulership of his heart.

However, the apostles of this Messiah-King also know of an enfeebled state of conscience, in which the conscience is influenced from another side and chained to dead objects: an idolatrous conscience, one that is bound to idols. Even a believing conscience

can be critically weakened by the influence of other
spirits: those that are hostile to the Spirit proceeding
from God. Kings, foreign dictators, and other leaders
[*Führer*] arise to bind our consciences and lead us
away from Christ.

The conscience is always weak when it is bound
by an influence different from that of Jesus Christ. It
wavers and goes astray. It is wrong in its judgments.
It makes demands that have every appearance of
decisiveness and manliness and yet arise out of weakness: they do not represent things as they actually
are, they give no real help, they use weapons that are
injurious to life, they contradict truth in that they
contradict God's Word and the Spirit of Jesus Christ;
they are dead and lead to death.

A conscience that pays allegiance to the wrong
leader is bound to transgress constantly against the
will to life that characterizes the rulership of Christ.
This fact is most painfully clear in the case of all
who combine the name "Christ" with an alien name
and goal. In this futile undertaking, Christianity
today, more than ever before, is deprived of the spirit
of him whom it still wants to confess. The pure Spirit
does not allow itself to be mixed with any other
spirit. His kingdom does not tolerate any rival power
structure.

What do idols and the house of God have in
common? Has goodness anything to do with
wickedness? Can the one join forces with the other
in the same undertaking? Does light associate with
darkness? When has the kingdom of God made an
alliance with a state built by human power? Did
Jesus ever mix other watchwords with his prophetic

2 Cor. 6:14–16

message? How can the word of Jesus tolerate rival human commands? When has God shared his sovereignty with human rulers? Can the city of God go hand in hand with Babel? Can one equate Christ and Belial, God and the devil?

Yet to hit out at a conscience that is sick and feeble does no good. Even an erring conscience deserves to be treated with consideration and respect. There must be some influence that frees it from all vacillating emotions and from all the ties of the antigod, without striking it dead to the ground. Surely there is a radiant light that overcomes all gloom and shadows. Faced with the rising sun, night is powerless. The Spirit that gives life is victorious over the spirit of murder. No other authority can bring peace. The Spirit of Life, the Spirit of Light, sets the conscience free. This Spirit conquers without destroying. God's rule takes command over the heart. The Spirit of his rulership transforms hearts and nations. The church of Jesus Christ here and now shapes an order of communal life with the same character as his future. The church's will to unity and her spirit of love transform everything. But they never kill anything that has life.

Rom. 8:2

Acts 2–4

Eph. 2:13–22

Unity gives the conscience assurance

The conscience is at peace only when it is in perfect accord with God's will. In the conscience of a believing and loving person, the will to truth dwells as the Spirit of Jesus. In this dark hour of world history, it is of crucial importance that this news, this answer, is carried to the four corners of the earth. Then the conscience will become free from all legalistic ties, from every influence of the zeitgeist, from every

human opiate, and from all demonic magic. The
distress in this hour demands a supreme strength – a
strength found only in the healing brought down to
mortally sick humankind by God's kingdom of life
and love. This mission goes out to every nation. The
task is clear. The message runs: "Let yourselves be
united! Unite in God! Unite with God!"

2 Cor. 5:19–20

Healing can be given only through community
with God in the redemption of his Christ. Without
God's justice, the conscience remains evil. Only
through faith in God has a good conscience any
stability, and this faith is given the most definite
confirmation in the unity of his church. All stimula-
tion from outside, all flames of human enthusiasm
that leap from one person to another, leave the
anxious question behind whether it was really God
who gripped the heart. There is only one criterion to
apply to this alarming question: the agreement of all
believers, the unanimity of their judgment, and the
full accord of their consciences in the tasks set before
them. The unity between the church and the words
and lives of the apostles and their prophecy is proof
that the voice speaking in human hearts is God's
voice. The conscience is robbed of all certainty if the
believers do not come to unity among themselves and
to unity with the life and spirit of the early church.
Certainty about the message leads to a uniting of the
believers, which is also a uniting with God.

John 17:20–26

Only from within can the conscience reach
this certainty. Community in all things is inmost
certainty. "The state of the conscience varies according to the degree of community with God and the
acceptance of his will. The closer the community

with God, the more does the conscience thrive."[13]
Only in this way is unanimity achieved. The more
deeply Christ dwells in our hearts the more sharply,
delicately, and carefully does the conscience insist
that truth means unity.

At first, what the kingdom of God demands
appears not only too sharp and strict but downright
impossible. But the perfect will of God gains recognition more and more as the will to joy, as the only
thing that is good and living. The more God's will
gains ground, the closer the conscience comes to
unity with God and his church. Therefore we can say
that when a conscience is healed it is in fact sharpened, purified, and clarified for the unity of complete
community. And further: the conscience loses its
clarity to the same degree as we refuse to serve the
will to unity. And finally: the conscience can never
give recognition to a church whose unity is not
constantly proved in deeds, or to a community supposedly in God that does not show a fitting attitude
and way of life. For basically the conscience is always
intent on action. God is action.

A right way of life shows, through the unity of
the church led by the Spirit, that it is in reality a
community in God. When the attitude of the believers is purified and unified through the Holy Spirit,
unanimity and unity of life come into being. In
Christ, their attitude to life becomes one with their
way of life. The conscience in its renewed sensitivity
strives toward this immediate goal, upholding the
influence of the Spirit of Jesus with unmistakable
certainty and perseverance.

---

13 Johann Adam Steinmetz, 1689–1762.

Faith and a good conscience are closely tied

As the moral function of the human spirit, the conscience has to say yes to everything that is prompted and inspired by the Spirit of God in the human spirit. In the human spirit, the conscience has to take a prophet's place – the place of one who is the mouthpiece of God and has to repeat and pass on what God says. The conscience that is on the way to recovery calls out, "God says it; God wills it; therefore it will come to pass." As the keenest instrument of the human spirit, the conscience has to represent in the liveliest way the uniting of the human spirit and the divine Spirit. God's Holy Spirit wants to unite with our spirit to witness to the truth together. Rom. 8:16 Our spirit's conscience will be clear and healthy to the same degree that our faith has accepted the Spirit of Jesus Christ.

When our conscience is on the way to recovery, the only attitude that will keep our inmost spirit pure and give it strength is the attitude that Jesus had. Keeping a good conscience depends entirely on keeping the holy faith. The redeeming and 1 Tim. 1:19 healing grace of God nurtures a purified and healed conscience in us. As a gift of this grace, faith denies godlessness in every thought, desire, and action. It denies all the worldly lusts that belong to godlessness and are harmful to life. Only in this way can we justly and with deliberation affirm the life of Jesus and accept it. We can do this only in community with God, that is, in community with his Holy Spirit.

Faith and a good conscience are so closely bound together that rejection of the one means shipwreck to the other. For this reason, baptism of faith testifies

1 Pet. 3:21 to the bond of a good conscience with God. The conscience is made good by faith. Without faith, it goes astray. It becomes a bad conscience. Therefore the apostles of Jesus Christ say about those who do not have faith that they are tainted in mind and Titus 1:15 conscience alike. This is inevitable because without faith the conscience has no anchor. And the opposite is just as true: if we ignore the compass of the Christ-directed conscience, the ship of faith will be dashed without warning on the next reef.

1 Tim. 6:12　　If we want to fight the good fight to the end, it is just as important to protect our faith as it is to protect our conscience. Faith in the freely given love of Jesus Christ needs to be treasured. A good conscience needs to be protected with the utmost watchfulness. True faith demands a tender and delicate conscience as a fruit of the Spirit. Faith gives birth to a death-defying and victorious decisiveness against all evil. Faith is served by a sound conscience. Faith demands deeds of love. It is, in fact, love of God, love of Christ, and love of the Holy Spirit. When we take pains to keep our consciences free of offense before God and man at all times, then we are given growth and activity in the grace and knowledge of Jesus Christ. Our inner lives become anchored in God and in all the powers of his Spirit. Only love is without offense.

Jesus purifies our consciences continually
Yet we should not make the mistake of thinking that when our conscience steadily gains health and purity in love, we become sinless! Sinfulness remains characteristic of our nature. But the grace of his blood – the grace of the sacrificed life of

Jesus – continually purifies our conscience through
the Holy Spirit. Again and again, grace purifies the
conscience from all dead works and all offensive
actions, from everything that violates the justice
and love that go hand in hand with faith. The Spirit
of Jesus Christ leads believers to a life that steadily
increases in clarity. And yet the believer continues to
be bound to all humankind by a common guilt.

Nevertheless, however clearly it shows itself to
be common to all people, the guilt *has* been wiped
out. We have the freedom to do good and to further
it, to avoid evil and to fight it. Step by step, there
is an advance toward the kingdom of God. In the
life of Jesus, sacrificed for us and brought near to
us, God has freely given us the gift that takes one
burden after another from our conscience. It makes
us free, without making us sinless. We become – not
gods – but people who allow the kingdom of God to
come to them.

We can accept God's will in our life only when we
are freed from the curse of a bad conscience. We can
be one with God's holiness only when our hearts are
unburdened, sprinkled, and consecrated. The heart   Heb. 10:19–22
is in a condition to come before God and become
united with him only by being in touch with the sacrificed life of Christ in the closest and most intimate
way, by being met by Christ himself and being united
with him as he was and is and will be. Therefore there
is no entry into the holy of holies except through the
blood of Jesus: Christ's stainless life, his dedicated
soul, his sacrificed body, and his quickening Spirit
unite us with God – the whole Christ with all the
power of his life and death.

John 14:6   Jesus is the way to God. There is no other God than the one who is the God and Father of Jesus. Wherever we may seek him, we find him in Jesus. Unless we are freed in Jesus from all our burdens, we try in vain to draw near to the Father as he is brought near to us by the Son. We have no access to God without forgiveness of sin. Jesus gives it to us by sacrificing his life – by sacrificing his body, his soul, and his blood.

    Through Jesus, Satan, the accuser of our brothers,
Rev. 12:10 is silenced. The conscience, too, is no longer allowed to accuse. Even the most murderous accusations that human blood can raise are stilled. The blood of the murdered brother, Abel, has been erased. The better blood of the new brother of man speaks louder
Heb. 12:24 than his. The blood of humankind has found a new representative and leader; by him, the better one, it is
Heb. 9:13–14 absolved and liberated. Murdered like Abel, he nevertheless speaks *for* his murderers instead of *against*
Luke 23:34 them. He, the guiltless one, has become one of them, because he is the only one who has become truly theirs. If he, the Son of Man, is for them, no one can condemn them. From now on, no accusation has the power to prevent them from approaching God.

    In Christ, the conscience that used to be our enemy becomes our friend. Previously, it had to condemn our life; now it says yes to the new life given to us in Christ. Freed from all impurity through community with him, the human spirit accepts the assurance and certainty given in Jesus Christ. So the conscience, as a Christ-conscience, becomes a representative of God. It becomes the voice of the one who is sent, representing our covenant with God. In the inner land of our soul, the conscience begins to do its task. In the church, our covenant with God comes into force. In the task of mission, the embassy steps forward to appear before the world.

The church has the authority of Jesus

It is the church that in baptism confirms the covenant of a good conscience with God. The believ-   1 Pet. 3:21
ers are united by the bond of faith, and baptism is the banner and battle flag of this unity of faith in the face of the whole world. There is no such thing as baptism without the church. The water of baptism is the pure water of the Spirit of Unity, just as the wine of the Lord's Supper proclaims the unity of the pure blood. Nor without the church is there any such thing as a meal celebrating unity of conscience. The common meal of love and thanksgiving confesses and proclaims the new covenant: the sure victory of unity given through the life and blood of Christ. The bread and the wine in remembrance of Jesus Christ are living symbols of the unity that has made many grains and many grapes into one whole. Only on the basis of the church can community be built up in the unanimity of all consciences. Only from the church can there be sent into the world a mission that is authenticated before all people in their consciences. From the church, unity will be proclaimed as God's freedom. Where her Spirit is, there is freedom.   2 Cor. 3:17

It was to the unity of the church, that is, to the unity of the apostles, that Jesus gave his Spirit with full authority to represent his kingdom. Their   Matt. 28:18–20
authority to loose and to bind, that is, to forgive and   Matt. 16:19
leave unforgiven, makes it possible for people to be

completely freed so that they can enter the kingdom of God. No conscience can live without forgiveness of sins. No one can see the kingdom of God without it. United in faith and in life, the church of God is entrusted with the power to forgive the sins of all consciences; she is given the life of Jesus and his future rule as her charge and prerogative for this day and age.

Acts 2:38

Acts 5:31
Eph. 1:7
Col. 1:14

False prophecy forgives without authority. Such forgiveness is null and void because it changes nothing in a person's life. Peace is proclaimed where there is no peace. Freedom is proclaimed where everything remains unfree. What is unjust is called just. The joyless are comforted with counterfeit joy and stolen happiness. Unity and community are betrayed. In the atmosphere of false prophecy, the conscience becomes dull and blunt and loses its commission. False prophecy robs the conscience of every sure footing from which to launch its attack.

Jer. 6:14

Yet where the truth of the Spirit of God proclaims forgiveness and peace, the conscience will be roused to constantly increasing action. It advances to the attack: where there was no peace, peace must be made; where everything was in chains, freedom must dawn; where injustice ruled, justice must take its place; where love and joy had grown cold, the joy of love breaks through; and where each one lived for himself, community comes into being. An all-out campaign against evil is launched: no area of life can escape being attacked. Resistance breaks down. The conscience of the world wakes up. The conscience of the church is on the march.

The Spirit-filled conscience becomes active

The prerequisite for this missionary attack is the effective working of consciences in the heart of the church. All growth in the gifts of God, every task given by his truth, and every deepening of community with him sharpens the conscience and intensifies its activity. In the presence of Jesus, we get to know ourselves more and more clearly and judge ourselves more and more firmly. The longer we go the way of the church, the more we know ourselves dependent on forgiving grace. The fact that in the church the conscience gains equally in tenderness and in strength is proof of the working of God in our midst. **Heb. 13:18** The conscience not only condemns and puts away everything that offends against love and community, however small or subtle, but even attacks all weariness and neglect. It punishes all dead works, for they actually prevent the Spirit of God from filling our hearts with the breath of life.

As long as God's Spirit is at work in his church among the believers, consciences work and speak without respite and without delay. A conscience that **Rom. 9:1** is as still as the grave is not a good conscience. Everything would be lost if this voice were to fall silent. It is only by a twofold deception that false prophecy can bring the conscience to the point of being deathly quiet. First of all, the conscience is lost when we allow ourselves to be persuaded to the false belief that evil and all consequent injustices are unchangeable – that their supremacy is inviolable. Educated to false humility in the face of evil and to false submission to alien gods, the conscience gives up the struggle and forfeits its fighting spirit. The god of this world and its zeitgeist has dazzled the conscience: he has cheated it of its goal.

If there is anything more dangerous than this submission to the influence of evil over the world, it is the second deception practiced by false prophecy: soothing the conscience with feigned self-assurance. It is another weapon, just the reverse of the first, but it is the same enemy. It attacks the front from the other flank. Through a morbid, imagined holiness it leads to the same result: the blunting and deadening of the conscience. Our conscience is inevitably struck dumb as soon as we see ourselves as sanctified and our own life as equal to Christ's. With such delusions we are further than ever from God's kingdom. Being self-satisfied, we no longer have the hunger and thirst without which there can be no God-given life among people, without which the righteousness of his kingdom cannot reach us. In both types of deception, there is a deadly similarity in the end: we belong to those who are seared, as it were, with a branding iron and hardened to their own conscience.

Among the personal testimonies through which Paul gives us a glimpse into his inner life as an apostle, the most striking is that his conscience too did not rest: through the free gift of God, Paul's conscience became as active as it was good. Because of the lively activity of his conscience, it was made free of all offense through grace. The testimony of Paul's conscience is confirmed by the simplicity and sincerity of everything this apostle of Jesus Christ does and says. This happens through the grace of God. The grace of God makes the one who is sent out able to carry out his commission among people. No human strength or wisdom can carry it out.

1 John 1:8

Matt. 5:6

1 Tim. 4:2

2 Cor. 1:12

The Crucified One frees us from guilt

It is forgiving grace that frees us undeserving people from all guilt. Only this grace can give an active conscience the help that protects and strengthens it. Only by being acquitted can a prisoner find new freedom for his work in life. It is the same today before the judgment bar of the conscience as it will be on the day of judgment at the end of history: only one thing will lead to release and acquittal – grace that forgives through the blood of the Crucified One, exoneration from all guilt through the deed of the Innocent One who was put to death.

This undeserved gift of an acquittal is given, not because of anything in the conduct or the inner life of the accused, but as a final, judicial pardon from the highest power. The life and blood, spirit and soul of Jesus must be accepted by the condemned and must become part of their very nature. Only in this way can they expect new life instead of death. Only in accepting the life and death of Jesus do they escape the death that their own lives deserve.

John 8:36

This exchange of life and death is nothing like the physical transfusion of actual blood, in which the ebbing life of one person is replenished by the blood of another – the rich, invigorating blood of the stronger transfused into the veins of the weaker. The soul and life of human blood is all the help humans know outside the gospel of Jesus Christ. It is quite different with Christ. With him, it is not created matter that is decisive but the Spirit of the Creator. There is no transfusion of a material substance here: it is not blood that is given to blood but spirit that is given to spirit. The Spirit, who is God, comes to the human spirit, which is not a material thing but life from God.

John 15:26–27

Jesus lived in the Spirit of God. He brought his kingdom in this Spirit. At the climax of his life, his soul, filled with the Holy Spirit, was poured out for us. This pure life of Jesus is the starting point from which his quickening Spirit streams out to the human spirit. The Crucified One gave his Spirit into the hands of the Father. From the Father, he sent out the Holy Spirit to his church. Now he who is Lord and Ruler is the Spirit of the church. In the Spirit, Christ imparts himself to us. Through this Spirit, we no longer lead our own lives but his life, and his life alone.

In this Spirit, Jesus is in the midst of those who believe in him. In this Holy Spirit, he is present with everything he has accomplished by his life and death. In this Spirit, strength comes to us – that strength with which he shattered all the instruments and weapons of death and exterminated all the poisons and germs of evil. The historical reality of the deed that blotted out all guilt brings us strength through the Holy Spirit.

From the death of Christ we receive the strength to break with things as they are and to die to the dead life within us and around us. This dying requires the utmost strength. It is given to us in Jesus. Then in all we are and do, what is decisive is no longer our life, or the life of others, but his life alone. Whatever we were and did before, we are now absolved and pardoned. Where the old life has come to an end, the new life begins.

The gift of purification of the conscience through the death of Christ brings the inner life into community with God. The Holy Spirit brings this about. In faith, the innermost soul has access to God. The believing spirit experiences the nearness of Jesus

Luke 23:46

John 14:17–18

John 16:7–13

Rom. 6:18–23
Gal. 6:15

Christ. Our spirit brings its witness into agreement
with the Spirit of God. Our conscience lives in the
Holy Spirit from now on. The Spirit of God leads our
spirit and its conscience. Christ proves himself as
the Risen One and the Living One in the powerful
working of his Spirit. Through him, the new life that
corresponds to the kingdom of God is brought into
being in and around us. This life demands a supreme
strength. It is given to us in Christ, the Living One.

Rom. 8:14–16

Christ transforms everything

In the Spirit of Jesus Christ, the kingdom of God
as justice, peace, and joy spreads over the whole of
life. All who believe in God in this way are able to
exert themselves to keep their consciences alive and
preserved from offense at all times before God and
man. When we have turned resolutely and steadfastly
away from evil, we can turn again and again to loving
justice and to peacemaking unity – to the purity and
truth of God's kingdom. This life in Christ is possible.
Wherever people believe in Jesus Christ, it will be
given through the Holy Spirit.

Rom. 14:17

Acts 24:16

Once it is bound to Christ, the conscience has
found its goal and its destiny. In the word and
example of Mary's Son, the picture of the longed-for
justice and righteousness engraved on the hearts of
all people finds its perfect original. In his work it has
found its consummation. This holy truth does not
want to remain outside the conscience. The life and
work of Jesus is planted into our hearts and all we do.
The person of faith becomes a living letter from Jesus
Christ; the truth of Jesus has become an inner word
written on the pages of the human heart.

Gal. 2:20

2 Cor. 3:2–3

Deeds are what make this handwriting legible to everyone – deeds that are imprinted on a life as they spring from the heart, one letter of the Spirit after another. The conscience is made clear and new, in that the holiness of God's will is alive in every heart and becomes a reality in every deed. The indwelling Christ illuminates our whole life. He transforms every sphere of our life from within to without. He makes

Rom. 7:6   everything new and different. The soul has received the truth into its innermost depths, into its spirit.

The conscience honors the truth by being obedient to it and gaining support from it. The conscience can be compared to a tender climbing plant: without a support it sprawls on the ground and withers. It needs something high and strong. But no matter what it climbs on, it does not change its nature. Ivy never adopts the form of leaf and growth of the tree it clings to in order to live. And yet its laborious climbing serves to glorify the object to which it is attached. Its destiny is that of the object it clings to. Should the tree fall, the ivy is inevitably involved in its fall.

The conscience seeks the Rock that cannot fall and can never change. It seeks God. It longs for Christ; it presses on toward his Spirit and his truth. It can never find peace and stability in other ideals, especially when they whip up emotional enthusiasm to the point of bloodlust. Certainty of conscience dwells in absolute truth alone.

Within itself, the conscience has no guarantee that it is right. It is like a pair of scales that has no weights. Given false weights, the more accurate and sensitive the scales are, the bigger the lie will be. It is more deceptive to weigh with false weights than to lie and deceive in other ways. Only true weights give the conscience any value. Without them it keeps on vibrating and wavering unsteadily, deceiving and misleading in the most dangerous way. Only absolute truth gives the conscience any authority or guarantee of being right. The truth and what the truth demands in life is all that the conscience can represent with confidence.

Truth gives the conscience clarity in politics
Medieval Germany's secret Vehmic courts, as well as doing some good, did untold harm. What they lacked was the clear foundation of an authoritative standard that had been objectively determined. We have experienced what confusion of conscience is caused by contradictory orders and their unforeseeable consequences, even when they have been issued by well-meaning governments and authorities. The most carefully thought-out legislation is pernicious if it cannot prove itself before the conscience to be an objective expression of absolute justice.

The horrors of these Vehmic courts have been directly brought home to us by the murderous commands of courts-martial, by the unbelievable opinions of excited reporters, by the appalling injustice of misinformed journalists, and by the confusing slogans of fanatical parties and civil war organizations.[14] The assassinations of our day are no mere coincidence. They have revealed the evil spirit of our time. Fanaticism is uncertainty run amok. That is the only reason

---

14 Arnold deliberately uses the term *Femgerichte,* or Vehmic courts, a medieval tribunal system of Westphalia which acquired the connotation of a lynch mob, to describe his own day. Right-wing political homicides of the early Weimar Republic were frequently called *Femmorde* by the media.

why it loses its head in senseless and exaggerated hate. It has forfeited all light and warmth. It has no heart. The conscience has lost its standard. Without any objective reason, it rages against everything that goes counter to its morbid obsessions.

In the great election fights of 1932, one man had to be taken to a mental hospital as a result of his desperate efforts to make up his mind in the utter confusion of his political ideas. That was more than a grotesque and isolated incident. He had made the daring attempt to go along with the convention policies of all parties and all factions. It may well be that he was more sensible and reasonable than the blind mass of voters. How much weaker are the consciences of those who cast their vote without ever having recognized the real nature of their party candidates and party platforms! How many there are who make no attempt to investigate the policy or motives of the party that is overthrown by their vote! People throw their votes into the scales of world history without being able to weigh up one party against the other. Conscience has been thrown to the winds. People have incurred responsibility for incalculable guilt. Without looking for guidance from their consciences, they have presumed to make weighty decisions over the destiny of whole peoples.

The conscience warns us: do nothing without sufficient reason; never act without a firm basis of fact; go into action only when you know what you are doing! The only way to safeguard our lives from the curse of irresponsible action is to accept the unfalsified weights – truth. The living code of God's justice inscribed on our hearts is the sole norm that must

Acts 4:19

guide all our decisions. Otherwise there is no ground under our feet. When God's nature – his unchangeable righteousness – is firmly imprinted on our conscience, then, and only then, can our conscience pass judgment and give witness.

Conflicting human opinions of relative right and relative wrong do not help the conscience toward well-founded decisions. It can take a clear stand only through the weight of God's truth. Only on the rock of the genuine Christ does the conscience find any stability. Christ alone is the example, guide, and liberator; he alone gives the conscience the foundation, the basis, and the reason for responsible action. There is no other righteousness than that of his coming kingdom.

Acts 5:29

Everything else varies, for it is uncertain. It changes its nature, for it is inadequate. It fluctuates, for it has no stability, no adequate foundation. Even in the best families and the finest schools, human ideas totter and fall. Everything that is human fluctuates between limp docility and rigid opposition. Nothing is certain. Everything is relative. The result is clear: in this relativism, which gives equal recognition to quite irreconcilable opposites, humankind loses all sense of values.

Jesus Christ remains the same forever

In the face of all this confusion, Jesus Christ remains today and forever exactly the same as he was in the time of Augustus and Herod and Pilate, no matter how many thousand times his clear picture is changed and falsified by this relativism. What his will brings about today is exactly the same as he will

Heb. 13:8–9

establish in his final kingdom at the end of time. Only he who is immutable is decision – everything else is delay and displacement. The relativism and fickleness of human opinions can have only one result: the will to live sickens and breaks down. Life gains health only through the absoluteness of Christ's will, which

Rev. 1:8

is always and forever the same. Health is strength to act and power to create, born out of a sure instinct for life and out of well-considered decisions. It calls for something firm and constant to fill the whole of life.

The conscience will become healthy only when it is completely bound to Christ. True life is not to be found anywhere else than in this divine influence, which is immutable. Only when Christ has become the anchor for our consciences, with no qualifications, can life recover. The distress of our time can be tackled only when our inner life regains health in Christ. The conscience looks to Christ for healing. It is Jesus who heals the people of our day and age just as he healed the sick in his day. It is Christ who shows our generation the way of salvation. It is the same way along which he, the king chosen by God,

John 14:6

will lead everything to the goal at the end of all days. The tremendous tasks facing us today can never be accomplished by the hopelessly confused spirit of our times but only by the Spirit of the future, the Spirit of Christ's kingdom.

Christ's Spirit of the future wants to be the Spirit of community here and now just as in the early

John 16:13

church. In the living Christ of the prophets and apostles the stream of future riches comes to us. It is in the apostolic word that Christ comes to us. It is in the prophetic word that his Spirit purifies our conscience.

He wants to submerge us in the truth as in a bath of invigorating waters. In the spirit of the prophets and apostles, the Spirit of Jesus Christ reveals himself always and everywhere as unchangeably one with himself. What he instills into our conscience today is no less than the substance of this constant accord with himself. He brings unanimity to the church today in one and the same way as to the prophets and apostles and to the church in all ages, inscribing on their hearts the one way of truth and of life.

John 17

In all ages, the Spirit of Jesus Christ proclaims the same things of the future. He brings the powers of the same future world to all generations. All those who accept these powers are able to live by them at all times. The Spirit constantly reminds us of the eternally valid words that Jesus Christ uttered. They can and shall be carried out by all generations on earth. The conscience of all believers becomes firm and sure through the direct uniting with the word of this Spirit, which is spoken into the conscience and is always the same as the word of the apostles and prophets. In this supreme unity, the conscience is equal to any new and unexpected event.

The conscience becomes lively and firm through this Spirit, who glorifies Christ as the unchanging Lord in the entire church of all times: past, present, and future. Out of faith, the Spirit of God awakens courage in us to do unflinchingly what this Spirit wants done. In this way, faith becomes joy in fruitful work and activity. This work corresponds to the kingdom of the same Christ who was and is and is to come.

Luke 8:15

A Spirit-filled conscience glorifies Christ

In the very beginning, the conscience got its voice from the vital fact that the first man was a living soul whose breath came from God. Since the fall of the soul, the conscience can do justice to this divine origin only when the last man, Jesus, as the quickening Spirit, has taken possession of the person

1 Cor. 15:45–47 whose soul is slowly dying. The old conscience – the conscience given to every human soul by nature – is by no means an authority for the apostolic task. Paul, the apostle of Jesus Christ, bases his witness on his

Rom. 9:1 conscience being in the Holy Spirit.

The witness Paul uses to prove the truth of his statements is not a divided one. On the contrary, the uniting influence of the holy, quickening Spirit heals the conscience that stands before God from all the dividedness it has fallen into through the corruption of the soul. God's Spirit purifies the human spirit to such a clarity that the one can unite with the other to make one witness. In the Holy Spirit, the conscience regains health to form a unanimous witness with this Spirit which is above all other spirits, the Spirit of God.

When the conscience lives in the Holy Spirit, it is so completely immersed in the Spirit that it breathes no other air than that of the Spirit. From then on, the nature and character of this Spirit determines the conscience. As a conscience in the Holy Spirit, it glorifies Christ, brings to mind all that Jesus said, and

John 14:26–27 leads to the active expectation of his future. In this way, the conscience rouses people to a most intent

Eph. 6:18 watching and praying so that they might not succumb

Matt. 26:41 to other spirits in times of danger nor be tempted

Mark 13:36 again by foreign influences to a new downfall. To fall again would mean not only the loss of their living soul but also the loss of the quickening Spirit.

Yet this Spirit is stronger than all other spirits. The sole purpose of the Holy Spirit in waking and protecting the conscience is to win a conclusive victory over all the powers that enslave people. The Spirit is at work when Christ is glorified, when God is revealed, and when his rule is recognized. God's power liberates the conscience from all other spiritual powers. No one but God himself, the Omnipotent, can win this victory.

1 John 5:4

1 Cor. 15:56–57

When the original Greek speaks of "the conscience that is bound to God," it relates the conscience so firmly and closely to God that to be accurate we would have to translate it as "God's conscience." The inner life senses this: "the conscience that is bound to God" is a conscience before God, toward God, and in God, a conscience of the Spirit of Jesus Christ, God's conscience. In God and through Christ, it has become free from every false direction and from every tie that enslaves. It lives in God and has become God's. God is the freedom of the conscience.

1 Pet. 2:19

Rom. 6:17–22

God's rule sets the conscience free

Today when all the impassioned movements among peoples take their stand in the struggle for freedom, what they have in mind is one of the ultimate thoughts of God's will. Freedom is God's thought for humankind. Without freedom, we are not yet fully human. Yet people are free only when they are not compelled to do what goes against their conscience. Emancipation gives back to the conscience the possibility of working without restrictions. We can speak of freedom only when life as an integrated whole asserts the freedom to fulfill its destiny in every area, spiritual and material.

A life is free only when it is lived in accordance with the deepest and ultimate calling. This applies not only to religion and morals (the more specific area of the soul's activity) but also to public relationships in society and economic life; not only to the innermost life of faith but also to vocational life and family life. The last battle for freedom is waged for a conscience that embraces all aspects of life. Any other fight for freedom is a delusion. Any restriction of the goal of freedom brings bondage. The German people has had teachers who taught freedom, and so it ought to know this truth: true freedom consists in the unhindered development of the full destiny of the whole human being. Freedom lives in wholeness.

Today there are voices calling for people to join together to fight the threat of a permanent subjugation of the "German spirit" and of "German labor." But right at the start of this, the foremost priority must be to attain clarity about the destiny of the human spirit, a destiny for an all-embracing freedom of conscience. Only then will it be possible to undertake anything that will lead to freedom. Before one hurries to devote oneself to a task, one must first know what the task is.

The call to freedom must mean freedom for everything that a healthy conscience wants; otherwise it is a lie and a delusion. We must know what we are freed *for* before we can be told what we must be freed *from*. The question is, *"Free for what?"* Freedom without a goal is bondage. What must become free is the will for the good; what it must become free for is good deeds. It is the purpose and meaning of a deed that make it good. A conscience cannot be called to freedom as long as it is lying bare and fallow, aimless and empty. Truth alone will make us free. Only the task that truth sets us gives meaning to our free dedication. Half-truths are untruths. The tasks they ask of us are worthless. Only the whole truth is freedom. John 8:32

It is essential to put aside all dependence on human beings and human standards if we want to fight through to the freedom of our ultimate destiny. Only this freedom gives purpose and meaning to our conscience. To the healthy conscience, voluntary subjection to human powers is bondage, for it demands a dedication that is in fact purposeless and truly meaningless. The apostle Paul challenges us to never again become slaves. Only in the one freedom, the freedom for which Christ has freed us, can we throw off once and for all the servitude that apes freedom and the slavery that hides beneath a mask. The obedience that springs from faith in Christ is freedom. It leads to a life that is in harmony with the holy "thou shalt" that comes from the healthy conscience. God's holy "thou shalt" is our holy freedom. It is the true essence of our soul and conscience. Gal. 5:1

Jesus Christ is the only leader [*Führer*] who leads to freedom. He does not bring a disguised bondage. He does nothing against the free will of the human spirit. He rouses the free will to do that (and only that) which every truth-loving conscience must urge it to do. "The Lord is the Spirit, and where the Spirit of the Lord is, there is freedom." Freedom is the free power for free action. 2 Cor. 3:17

Anyone who wants to hand over the responsibility for his own actions to a leader [*Führer*] – anyone who wants to obey a human leader – has betrayed freedom.

He has become the slave of a human being. His enslaved conscience will be brought to utter ruin if this mis-leader calls to a freedom that is no freedom. All leaders whose authority is merely human ruin people's consciences. It is for this reason that Jesus said: "You shall not call each other leader [*Führer*].

Matt. 23:8   Only one is your Master, but you are brothers." The foundation of freedom on which the conscience can regain health is brotherliness and equality before God. This alone guarantees that love – the pure love

Gal. 5:6, 13   that springs from faith – is put into practice.

The freedom of the church means healing and health for the conscience. This freedom is given by the only Spirit that is free: the Spirit of God. It is God's rule that brings freedom to the conscience. The kingdom comes. The healing of all hurt begins. The conscience that is bound to God becomes free and healthy. Then it becomes active – then the way is cleared. Work begins. The whole of life becomes free. The work of the Spirit is established. The

John 8:36   person who is made free by Christ is indeed free. The freedom of Christ masters reality. Through Christ, the conscience becomes healthy in this freedom that comes from clear and objective decisions. Then creative powers arise as a result of this instinctively sure way of life. The conscience has found substance and meaning in the will of the Spirit. The healing of humankind is the kingdom of God.

Other Titles by Eberhard Arnold

God's Revolution
Justice, Community, and the Coming Kingdom
Excerpts from talks and writings on the church,
family, government, world suffering, and more.

The Early Christians
In Their Own Words
This collection of early Christian writings challenges
readers to live more fully and radically.

Why We Live in Community
with two interpretive talks by Thomas Merton
A time-honored manifesto on the meaning and
purpose of community.

Salt and Light
Living the Sermon on the Mount
Thoughts on the "hard teachings" of Jesus
and their applicability today.

The Prayer God Answers
Rediscover the kind of prayer that has the power
to transform our lives and our world.

Plough Publishing House
PO BOX 398, Walden, NY 12586, USA
Robertsbridge, East Sussex TN32 5DR, UK
4188 Gwydir Highway, Elsmore, NSW 2360, Australia
845-572-3455 • info@plough.com • *www.plough.com*